The Tale of
Jemima Puddle-Duck

The Tale of Jemima Puddle-Duck

by Beatrix Potter

 THE CLASSIC

What a funny sight it is to see

a brood of ducklings with a hen!

—Listen to the story of

Jemima Puddle-duck, who was annoyed

because the farmer's wife would not

let her hatch her own eggs.

Her sister-in-law,

Mrs. Rebeccah Puddle-duck,

was perfectly willing to leave

the hatching to some one else —

"I have not the patience to sit on

a nest for twenty-eight days;

and no more have you, Jemima.

You would let them go cold;

you know you would!"

"I wish to hatch my own eggs;
I will hatch them all by myself,"
quacked Jemima Puddle-duck.

She tried to hide her eggs;
but they were always found and carried off.

Jemima Puddle-duck became quite desperate.

She determined to make a nest right away from the farm.

She set off on a fine spring
afternoon along the cart-road
that leads over the hill.

She was wearing a shawl
and a poke bonnet.

When she reached the top of the hill,
she saw a wood in the distance.

She thought that it looked
a safe quiet spot.

Jemima Puddle-duck was not much
in the habit of flying. She ran downhill
a few yards flapping her shawl,
and then she jumped off into the air.

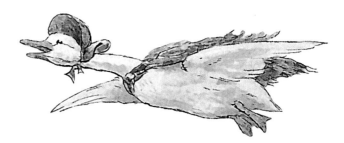

　　She flew beautifully when

she had got a good start.

　　She skimmed along over the tree-tops

until she saw an open place in

the middle of the wood,

where the trees and brushwood

had been cleared.

Jemima alighted rather heavily,
and began to waddle about in search of
a convenient dry nesting-place.
She rather fancied a tree-stump
amongst some tall fox-gloves.

But—seated upon the stump,
she was startled to find an elegantly
dressed gentleman reading a newspaper.

He had black prick ears and
sandy coloured whiskers.

"Quack?" said Jemima Puddle-duck,
with her head and her bonnet
on one side —"Quack?"

The gentleman raised his eyes
above his newspaper and looked
curiously at Jemima —

"Madam, have you lost your way?"
said he. He had a long bushy tail
which he was sitting upon,
as the stump was somewhat damp.

Jemima thought him mighty civil
and handsome. She explained that
she had not lost her way,
but that she was trying to find
a convenient dry nesting-place.

"Ah! is that so? indeed!" said the gentleman
with sandy whiskers, looking curiously
at Jemima. He folded up the newspaper,
and put it in his coat-tail pocket.

Jemima complained of the superfluous hen.

"Indeed! how interesting!

I wish I could meet with that fowl.

I would teach it to mind its own business!

But as to a nest—there is no difficulty:

I have a sackful of feathers in my wood-shed.

No, my dear madam, you will be

in nobody's way. You may sit there

as long as you like,"

said the bushy long-tailed gentleman.

He led the way to a very retired,

dismal-looking house amongst the fox-gloves.

It was built of faggots and turf,

and there were two broken pails,

one on top of another, by way of a chimney.

"This is my summer residence;

you would not find my earth

—my winter house—so convenient,"

said the hospitable gentleman.

There was a tumble-down shed at the back
of the house, made of old soap-boxes.
The gentleman opened the door,
and showed Jemima in.

The shed was almost quite full of
feathers—it was almost suffocating;
but it was comfortable and very soft.

Jemima Puddle-duck was rather surprised
to find such a vast quantity of feathers.

But it was very comfortable;
and she made a nest without any trouble at all.

When she came out, the sandy whiskered gentleman was sitting on a log reading the newspaper— at least he had it spread out, but he was looking over the top of it.

He was so polite, that he seemed almost sorry to let Jemima go home for the night. He promised to take great care of her nest until she came back again next day.

He said he loved eggs and ducklings; he should be proud to see a fine nestful in his wood-shed.

Jemima Puddle-duck came every afternoon;
she laid nine eggs in the nest.

They were greeny white and very large.

The foxy gentleman admired them immensely.

He used to turn them over and count

them when Jemima was not there.

At last Jemima told him that

she intended to begin to sit next day—

"and I will bring a bag of corn with me,

so that I need never leave my nest

until the eggs are hatched.

They might catch cold,"

said the conscientious Jemima.

"Madam, I beg you not to trouble
yourself with a bag; I will provide oats.
But before you commence
your tedious sitting, I intend to give you
a treat. Let us have a dinner-party
all to ourselves!"

"May I ask you to bring up some
herbs from the farm-garden to make
a savoury omelette? Sage and thyme,
and mint and two onions, and some parsley.
I will provide lard for the stuff—lard
for the omelette," said the hospitable
gentleman with sandy whiskers.

Jemima Puddle-duck was a simpleton:
not even the mention of sage
and onions made her suspicious.

She went round the farm-garden,
nibbling off snippets of all
the different sorts of herbs
that are used for stuffing roast duck.

And she waddled into the kitchen,

and got two onions out of a basket.

The collie-dog Kep met her coming out.

"What are you doing with those onions?

Where do you go every afternoon

by yourself, Jemima Puddle-duck?"

Jemima was rather in awe of the collie;

she told him the whole story.

The collie listened, with his wise
head on one side; he grinned when
she described the polite gentleman
with sandy whiskers.

He asked several questions

about the wood, and about the exact

position of the house and shed.

Then he went out,

and trotted down the village.

He went to look for two fox-hound

puppies who were out

at walk with the butcher.

Jemima Puddle-duck went up
the cart-road for the last time,
on a sunny afternoon.
She was rather burdened with bunches
of herbs and two onions in a bag.

She flew over the wood,

and alighted opposite the house of

the bushy long-tailed gentleman.

He was sitting on a log; he sniffed the air, and kept glancing uneasily round the wood. When Jemima alighted he quite jumped.

"Come into the house as soon as
you have looked at your eggs.

Give me the herbs for the omelette.

Be sharp!"

He was rather abrupt.
Jemima Puddle-duck had never
heard him speak like that.

She felt surprised, and uncomfortable.

While she was inside she heard

pattering feet round the back of the shed.

Some one with a black nose sniffed

at the bottom of the door, and then locked it.

Jemima became much alarmed.

A moment afterwards there were most awful noises—barking, baying, growls and howls, squealing and groans.

And nothing more was ever seen of that foxy-whiskered gentleman.

Presently Kep opened the door of
the shed, and let out Jemima Puddle-duck.

Unfortunately the puppies rushed in
and gobbled up all the eggs before
he could stop them.

He had a bite on his ear and both
the puppies were limping.

Jemima Puddle-duck was escorted

home in tears on account of those eggs.

She laid some more in June,

and she was permitted to

keep them herself: but only four of

them hatched.

Jemima Puddle-duck said that

it was because of her nerves;

but she had always been a bad sitter.

The Tale of Jemima Puddle-Duck
by Beatrix Potter

Published by The Classic Publishing Co.
© The Classic Publishing 2013
All rights reserved. No part of publication may be reproduced,
stored in a retrieval system, or transmitted, in any form or by any means,
without the permission of the copyright holder, The Classic Publishing Co.
Color art by The Classic Publishing Co.

The Classic in Mirbookcompany Publishing Co. Ltd.
239-18, Yeonnam-dong, Mapo-gu, Seoul, Korea
Telephone : 02-3141-4421 Fax : 02-3141-4428
Web site : cafe.naver.com/mirbookcompany
E-mail : sanhonjinju@naver.com